Hit Hard
Score High

Sevens Facts to be Healthy Rich and Happy

Neithe Soleyn

Dedications

*For I am not ashamed of the Gospel of
Christ: for it is the power of God unto
Salvation to everyone that believeth;
to the Jew first and also to
the Greek (Rom.1:16)*

*I dedicate this Memoir to
my Almighty Supreme Father
God, His Majestic Son Jesus Christ
and The Holy Spirit, who has
been my eternal giver and
sustainer of my life
and godly heritage.*

*To my deceased Parents, Percy and Flora
Michael, who have taught and inspired
me with spiritual and family values.
To my husband and all of my
children, my pastors, and
members at FAITH*

Acknowledgments

My sincere and great heartfelt appreciation to Jehovah God who has created his Spirit

within my being and has miraculously inspired me to write this volume.

To my children, Susan, Sharon, Stephern, Evangeline, Caroline, and Lawrence, my husband, all my Grandchildren and son- in-laws.

To FAITH'S Ministers; Roslyn Thorpe: Ruth MC Koy and Grace Harry, have encouraged me over the years to write this book and stated this was overdue for writing. Also, Rev. Greta Edwards and MC Koy assisted in encouraging the flock, even in hours of my hard labor.

Sister Mary Samuels, who has been so kind, desiring to assist me with my home chores, Brother Millington engaged in interview process.

Some of my fellow ministers in the Gospel of Christ, Rev. Norma Thompson and Rev. Dr. Daphne Cox.

The brethren of Faith Deliverance Pentecostal Church of God (FAITH), who has allowed me to shepherd them.

Contents

Preface

I honor our Heavenly Father, Son, and Holy Spirit for this great life. God is everything to me–without the Creator this script would not have existed. This Book HIT HARD SCORE HIGH: TRIUMPHANT OVER HARD TRIALS (With Seven Facts to Be Healthy, Rich, and Happy) is unique because of who I am. The contents of the manuscript might not be popular in some of my circles. I am a born-again Christian, a Pastor who is sanctified and filled with God's Holy Spirit. I have been moved to share some of my experiences with people, who are sometimes dying to hear how others have overcome what they are going through. My message to them is that they are not alone and they will make it safely through their journeys. The Bible declares; "Some made it safely to the shore, on broken pieces (Acts 27:44)." In this plot, the feelings of disappointment were present, but in fact neither of us were failures. God permitted our ordeals to fulfill God's purposes in our lives, for His own glory.

*For many years I have assisted many people with various needs that required answers. In this quest for responses, an untold number began to find help and others will benefit because I am a Servant of God who depends on His Holy Spirit for guidance, insight, wisdom, and strength. It is God Jehovah who has called me to serve and trust Him and has rendered unto me the grace to pass in times of testing. God's grace has allowed me to conquer at all times. As a result of my friend and I experiences, we **have been honored with rich knowledge.***

"Hit Hard Score High"

Triumphant Over Hard Trials
(With Seven Facts To Be Healthy, Rich, And Happy)

CHAPTER ONE

Prologue

You have the power to make it happen in your life. This book contains the true stories of my life and what people of all creeds, ethnicities, and religions have succeeded. The remedy of the principles that I have received is beyond the recommendation that is offered in many places. The stories, phases, and principles that I have written have derived from my own experiences, and might not be found in numerous manuscripts.

This volume is written for people who have had similar understandings to the ones that I have had and for those who have not. It is for mothers, wives, husbands, young people, the rejected, the incarcerated, and the enslaved. It is for the divorced, bereaved, singles, and educators, leaders of every magnitude, students, Christians, Jews, Muslims, and all groups and religions to find true help, peace, wisdom, power, love, success, and life everlasting.

I have shared some of my deepest stories with the world. You will find that the phases are things you are experiencing, or will incur. About ninety percent of the phases and principles, derived from my own experience through my healing process. There are powerful and life-changing principles to help you find a solution. This book is worth cherishing, reading, and applying to situations. The world in which we live is a great and wonderful place that our God has created for mortal man to dwell. Along the path in this life, there is sometimes joy, pain, gain, and loss. In all of these incidents, human lives are designed by God to overcome all adversity. Sometimes a life situation can hit you real hard. You can picture yourself being in a fight. In so many occasions, the battle can be pictured as a ball game a wrestling match. You must determine that whenever you are hit hard with unwanted situations of life, you will say to yourself, I am going to score high by God's grace and be triumphant over hard trials. We are responsible for the way in which we accept the changes in life. You can allow your minds to be stronger than your occurrences.

The Wrestling Match Idea

When I set out to write this book, I looked through some of my experiences in life, and I thought of several titles. After writing out some of them, I received a revelation for *Hit Hard Score High*, which means, "triumph over hard trials." A trial can be difficult to pass, if ones' faith is weak. Oftentimes, as human Beings we are afraid to encounter certain trials. In playing a ball game one cannot be afraid of facing their contenders. All individuals need an unwavering faith to fight in life's test. Immediately, after I had the title of the book-*Hit Hard Score High*, I recalled when I was a child and I saw men playing ball, there were two teams of men engaged in the game. Each time the team members made a hard hit and scored high, the spectators responded with loud shouts and cheers. At the end of the game the team which scored the highest points became the winner. On the other hand, the team members that did not score high in the same match were left defeated and saddened. Having some knowledge of the game, I set out to acquire a broader view.

I made an appointment to interview one of my parishioners who had the experience of being a football coach. I asked, "What does it mean for the person or team that loses a match?" He replied, "It causes mental and psychological pain, depression, and more. Sometimes doctors must be assigned to them for psychological, mental and physical care," I also learned that the team who suffers defeat can rise to power and victory after many hard practices.

In 1976, it was my first time to watch a boxing match on television. I will never forget the name of one of the boxers- were- Mohammed Ali. I remember how intelligently he avoided his opponent's punches and how, at the same time he seized every opportunity to hit his opponent and knock him to the ground. When he got him to the ground, Muhammad Ali would strategically cover his rival with his body for a while. It appeared very difficult for any challenger to arise from the ground. We should also know that in a boxing match that two boxers suffer challenges, and both are defensive.

Bill Walker in *Wrestling Rules, Scoring Criteria, and More*, writes, "The wrestler in control or on top is referred to as the offensive wrestler, while the other on the bottom is the defensive mat man…only the defensive man can score an escape or reversal (Walker. August 29, 2012) 3." The individual mat man who is pinned by his opponent has to fight bravely and skillfully to rise victoriously over his rival. In the case of the ball player, as badly as he is defeated, he refuses to let his failure cause him or the team to lose again. In return, they struggle for the victory and win. For so many of us, the fight is not on the ball ground or on the wrestling mat. The majority of our adverse situations may appear to be caused by other human beings. In my knowledge, people are not our real opponent. The devil is man's greatest enemy, of which many people might fail to realize. "The devil goes about like a roaring lion looking for anyone he can devour. We must avoid him in the faith (1Peter 5: 8)". In our life's journey, we are engaged in a fight, and this warfare is a spiritual fight. Since I was sixteen years old, I have had a spiritual encounter with Jehovah God that has changed my life and allowed me to look at my incidents as that to become stronger. I have learned in the scriptures that "We wrestle not against flesh and blood but it is against principalities, powers, and spiritual wickedness in high places." (Eph, 6:12)

People must be strong in their minds to press for success, after encountering any undesirable circumstances. They should take courage to succeed in their education, to make an unfinished residence habitable, and to earn extra income to survive financially when they are already employed in a job and pursuing higher education. On the other hand, growing a healthy child with little or no money, learning to keep a sound mind, and fighting to stay in the good fight, while making others happy; remaining in leadership position in stormy times is also difficult.

Missing a close friend or a partner with whom you shared life together, it hurts. It can become painful when your hope was set for a lasting confidant. Having the need for companionship and acceptance can cause your mind to be disturbed for a long time, if you are not careful to trust God's promise.

Many people are troubled because of the loss of a job, a better life style, innocently demoted from their position.

They are also saddened because they have lost their sex partner. In some cases they may have felt violated by their trust in that individual. They felt they made the wrong decision in committing themselves to an inappropriate sexual relationship. Or perhaps they were raped or coerced into the act.

The situation of losing an intimate friend, sex partner, the lack of shelter, food, and other matters can bring a great number of people into depression. Individuals have to be strong and knowledgeable to avoid the effects that can come with these losses. In many of these trying times, records have shown that drugs are administered for depression. Bob Murray and Alicia Fortinberry in *Fact Resources Sheet* affirms; "Standard antidepressants, such as Selective Serotonin Reuptake Inhibitors (SSRI), Prozac, Paxil, Zoloft, and Aropax are given for this disorder, which results in violence, suicide, brain tumors, and more (Fortinberry, Murray 10 Oct. 2012)."

People can also go into depression when hitting hard with failure in their pursuit for a better education. This matter is especially likely to happen when a student have been accepted into a program, with a very high score and have tried to avoid failure. Then surprisingly at the end of the Semester, the student was told, "You are on your own, and you are disapproved." You may feel like your world has crumbled beneath you, and you can be left shattered. Not only in ball games and wrestling matches can people rise to victory when *hit hard*. Undoubtedly, you can rise to higher ground and be triumphant over the anguishes of life. You can also avoid many lingering months and years of despair and live a healthy, rich, and happy lifestyle.

You can find health by following my principles. I did not allow myself the risk of pills. I found peace with the things that are written in this volume, because of God's mercies toward me. God must get the glory above any other thing. Almighty God has taught me to wrestle in order to possess a strong mind. This has allowed me to conquer the loss of a close friend, gain educational approval after being disapproved, assisted in finding shelter to generate income in a trying time, triumph over sexual desires, and lead in integrity in the midst of needs. I have learned to be determined each day to keep the peace of God in my heart and be content and happy. I have found life to be worth living in spite of my disappointments and humbling ordeals.

With much appreciation from Father God, I have received the ability to write this book.. My life has become an epistle that many people can read. The trial of losing a friend and other trials were not simple matters for me; these trying circumstances have allowed me to be strong and to help others become courageous, powerful, and successful. E.M Bounds States; in his writing in *The Best On Prayers*, "We need a quickening faith in God's power…God is not limited in action, nor controlled by man's infinite condition" (Bounds 1987, . 196)."

In the Worst of Times

I know what it means to feel like the heart was broken, when my close kin walked out from the residence and say goodbye. Immediately several feelings came upon me. I felt as though someone who was close to me was dead and was carried out of the shelter. I also experience head trauma, feelings of incapability, hurt, emptiness and resentment for a short time. All of these feelings came upon me, not realizing that I allowed myself to accept them. God's grace is limitless, and we can receive in abundance from our Lord. In all of these phases, the mercies and faithfulness of God's promise were extended to me. I felt so broken, because this intimate possessed good qualities.

The basic rules that I adopted are derived from my faith in God and my knowledge that God's Holy Spirit was with me in my trials. It is very important to return thanks, after we have received the things that we once needed. Dr. George Rekers, in *Family Building: Six Qualities Of A Strong Family* affirms, "We can convey kindness in giving of money, effort, time. He goes on to say that giving our money and time indicates our willingness and concern to share our goods (Rekers 1985, 290)".

This book covers ten chapters, including the preface. The preface explains why I wanted to write the book and its ultimate purpose. The prologue introduces the volume and gives educational and inspiring insights into what will be found within the ten chapters. Seven subjects are described as *facts*; these facts can also be seen in light of my stories. In this manuscript, the story is called *experience*. The story begins with a reference in some cases. These are arranged from chapters three through nine, and chapter ten gives a narrative of leadership. Under each account of the facts, there are phases and principles. Headings listed under *facts* include the following:

(I) Conquering the Loss of an Intimate Friend

(II) Turning an Abandoned House into Income

(III) Be an Honor Student, Even When Disapproved

(IV) Keeping a Sound Mind

(V) Conquering Sexual Desires If You Do Not Have a Partner

(VI) Raising a Baby with Little or No Income

(VII) Staying Engaged in the Good Fight and Making Others Happy

For the seven phases and seven principles, a subtitle is given for each phase and principle. Each phase is a combination of situations that occurred in the story. The principles, in most cases, are the solutions to the circumstances derived from the phases. Facts from the phases and principles include the following: Keeping a Sound Mind, Raising a Baby with Little or No Income, and Conquering Sexual Desires If You Do Not Have a Partner. These facts were given to me by revelation and knowledge as I entered into the experience. An example of *Fact I*:

Fact I

Phase 1: Feels Like a Dead Person Leaves the House

Principle 1: Find a Quick Source

Phase 2: Next Day Head Trauma

Principle 2: Dealing with the Ordeal

Phase 3: The Feelings of Resentment and Hurt

Principle 3: Reevaluating the Problem

Phase 4: Emptiness and Hurt

Principle 4: Forgiveness

Phase 5: Realizing the Long Hall and Blaming Others:

Principle 5: Compassion for the Lost.

Phase 6: Spirit and Self Are Quickened.

Principle 6: Using the Power of Faith

Phase 7: A New Life with Healing and Adjustment

Principle 7: Focusing on God, Making Others Happy.

As you read, study, and apply these elements you will discover that you are, in fact healthier than you realize, and may not need to be treated with medication, unless there is some uncontrollable matter. You will experience a healthy mind. According to *Phase 6*, your mind and spirit will be quickened. Apply the principle of faith; it is the key to obtaining power. The Bible speaks of "Faith is the quality of things, not seen, but still believes (Hebrews 11:1)". Trusting in God has given me the strength to work through this entire process. I was faced with hard trials, but I believed God and his word and kept on pressing for some things I did not physically see. With much determination, I had to go deeper to find everlasting peace. You have to push to become strong and useful during these times of hardship.

Instead of avoiding the problem, I fought against anything that hindered my recovery. Like many people, I never grew up having close friends. In choosing a confidant, I expected true and lasting years of friendship. My priority was always God, and the result was a healthy, rich and happy life.

CHAPTER TWO

Experience

Happiness is not only found in silver and gold. To a certain measure, you can have money and still live without happiness. This book will show you that I have been blessed to experience peace when I did not have money. I received the actual cash when I was down and out. You can enjoy life although you have been hurt, and you can rise above depression. You have to defend yourself in a godly fight.

The Resource Fact Sheet by Dr. Bob Murray, Alicia Fortinberry in *Resources Fact Sheet* shows that "there is a growing trend of adults yearly in the United States of America that have Depression Disorder at the age of age 18 and older. Preschoolers are the fastest growing with over one million. Depression is the second killer after heart disease (Murray, Fortinberry October 10, 2012)". Many different factors cause depression. These dynamics can be the loss of intimate friend, sexual and mental abuse, lack of shelter, food, jobs, money, and more. An intimate friend can be a kin in the person of a sister, spouse, neighbor, or another. Morris G. Watkins, Lois I. Watkins *The Complete Christian Dictionary For Home And School* define intimate as "marked by closeness in relationship, familiarity, intimate friends, personal and private and more" (Watkins, Watkins 1992, 359)."

Over twenty years ago, I was faced with several dilemmas. One of which involved an individual who became a closely friend. We first met each other at one of my family's residence in the early 1960s. We lived in the same vicinity. Living a Christian life was always my passion. My friend and I had shared the same faith of living for Christ. After ten months, our friendship became a bond.

In the early 1980s, my friend and I visited to the United States. In 1987, I became a founder of a Church. As a prime spiritual leader of an organization, mother, wife, friend, counselor and more. The relationship that I had with my friend appeared lost and ruined. Still, I knew that my friend intended to keep the comradeship. There are good qualities that reflect from this person's life. We both knew that the obstruction came from the Devil, but more over our Father God has designed a divine plan for our lives.

I learned to place trust in God's grace to have a better and lasting friendship. I devoted myself to making a connection by forgiving mistakes and forgetting past events, changing status, spending money, avoiding negative signs, and doing things together. Anything that is good is worth holding, and my friend was precious to me. I moved into an unfinished building that was once abandoned. During that time, I discovered a change that did not strengthen the relationship. In the early 1990s, I awoke one morning not realizing that it was going to be the beginning of a lost comradeship, a friendship that the Lord had helped me to hold for over many years. An incident had emerged that morning, without any verbal communication being exchanged. I heard my intimate say goodbye to those who were present with me. I held my composure. I did not react as though I were totally in distress. Meanwhile, I began to feel completely forsaken and cast off. That forsakenness felt like a terrible blow. I know I was *hit hard.* The feelings of head trauma, desertion, and other were a result of my own fears, and concerns. I acknowledge that our own fear can hurt us. Job the Patriarch in the *Bible* says; "The things I greatly feared has come upon me (Job 3: 25)". Sometimes, unconsciously we are over concerned of how communities will judge us in our struggles. I believed that people's judgment was one of my fears. As mortals, we are yet to understand, leaders are human beings and they will have trials. Nevertheless, I learned quickly, not to be afraid of anything, because God is sufficient to take us through any adversity.

I kept the scene of the departure in my mind and did not hold any discussion on that matter. The Lord whom I had served for many years sustained me through the night. I realized God had a great purpose for our lives. Says Dr. George Rekers in *Family Building: Six Qualities Of A Strong Family*; "There are three kinds of people, those who make things happen, those who watch things happen, and those who don't know things happen (Rekers 278)." That night I thought of so many sacrifices that had been made to keep the relationship strong. For these reasons, I fell into a state of sadness and felt I had really lost someone that I loved.

Like a Death Blow

The day after losing my friend, my brain felt packed and loaded with burden, disappointment, grief and confusion. I felt as though my forehead was about to explode, and if it did, my capacity for thinking would leave me. Two of the floors above me were just shells; no one else lived in the residence besides my immediate family unit. I opened my eyes and cried aloud, saying, "God! You promised to keep me in my right mind." I also continued in my regular prayer and praise to God. During the course of the day, I struggled through embarrassment, hurt and a sense of emptiness. The night of the second day, I fell asleep, and as

I awoke, the same feeling that was present in my forehead on the first morning was with me. I cried aloud and said the same words, "God, you promised to keep me in my right mind." I can clearly remember waking to daylight the third day; I was completely freed from the confused mind that was in disarray. I quickly realized my friend did not set out to hurt me, but the Lord allowed the experience for God's honor and Glory. Since then I refused to embrace certain thoughts and feelings. We must resist any thoughts and feelings that present bad outlook. Knowledge is power. "My people are destroyed, because of the absence of knowledge (Hosea 4:6)." It is important that we know the difference between right and wrong. The wrong thoughts we choose can bring us disasters.

Prayer is part of my lifestyle. The first thing that I do every morning when the Lord wakes me is to give praises; often I lift my voice loudly in praises for about an hour, after which I continue in intercessory prayer, thanksgiving and more. I knew without a doubt that my prayer life with Jehovah would get me to a better place in spite of the experience. My trust in God was unmovable, but I was hurting within. As the week advanced, I called my friend and I said, "If I have done anything wrong, I am sorry. Come back." I did not receive a reply, but I went so low as to reveal my priority for us to be together. It was the first major step in my recovery.

As a leader, it was hard to imagine teaching others about good and lasting relationships after mine had crashed terribly. About three weeks later, I was able to save myself from the blame of guilt and shame. I rescued myself from guilt and a certain amount of humiliation, because I prayed to God in Jesus' name.

My petition was, "Lord, if I did anything that was wrong to my friend to cause my suffering, please reveal it to me!" During my prayer in the first month to my Father God, I felt relief from blame and I felt deeply convinced that I did not do anything wrong to cause this disconnection. It was the second major step in my healing. I confessed that the Holy Spirit of God revealed to my spirit the guiltlessness of my suffering. Dr. George Rekers states, "The first prerequisite for effective crisis management is that the conscientious individual has a realistic insight of the event (Rekers 1987, 159)." Lack of awareness in a disaster can keep one in bondage to a situation. Four years later, without asking if I was the cause of the departure, my friend confessed to me that I did not do anything wrong to cause the disconnection. Thanks to God, I was already freed from my moments of doubt about the cause for my affliction.

Quickened In The Midst of the Ordeal

In about the second month of the ordeal, I thought that I would not have enough money to take care of my mortgage and to complete some carpentry work and other repairs on my residence. Immediately, I began thinking about joining two different lending hands program called Susu.

Having the vision to complete the house, a certain measure of strength filled and lightened my inner being. Immediately I was moved to action to find enough money to begin work. As I advanced with the repairs on the building, my courage and mind grew stronger. The hurt feelings over my situation hardly had any effect on my mind. By God's grace, I strove to quickly overcome a feeling that was very close to depression. Later on my friend helped faithfully to complete the residence.

Perseverance

There was no intention within me to retreat and give up. I kept on praying and said that my trials would be used to help many women and people in relationships.

Just before this situation arose, I was in the first semester of a five year college program. I suffered an illness that forced me to be hospitalized. I was very blessed to be able to function in class. At the end of the first semester, I did not receive credit for one subject due to my hospitalization, but I still received a 3.5 grade point average. Eight students, including me, were called to meet one of the school's personnel. We were told that we had met the school's requirements and that we were being given the privilege to become mentors in the college. I was *hit hard*, but I was blessed to *score high*.

I graduated from that college and then attended the Medgar Evers College in Brooklyn, New York some months later to take a few more courses. A year later I matriculated in a Masters program in science and administration and human recourses from the Audrey Cohen College known as Metropolitan College of New York.

God's Grace

My position as a spiritual leader was also put to the test. A spiritual or Christian leader is someone who the world looks to for guidance. Had it not been for my bond with God and his Son, Jesus Christ, I could have gone into depression. In the first couple of months, I believed that God by His Holy Spirit revealed two portions of scripture to me that became a tower of strength for my life. One of these scriptures was Luke 16:24: "If any man would come after me, let him deny himself, take up his cross and follow me." The other was, "We glory in tribulations also: knowing that trial works patience and endurance hope. Hope makes not ashamed for God's love is shed about in your hearts through Christ (Romans 5:3-5)." God's words came to me directly and forcefully.

I accepted the fact that the circumstance with my friend was a trial and that I must bear it with grace. This thought brought consolation and peace to my spirit. I refuted the thought that my rival's act should keep me pinned down. I was willing to use my spiritual skill and wrestle until victory was won. According to Romans 5:3-5, I was gaining patience and knowledge in my journey, which resulted in allowing me to help others. I confessed that what I was going through was for a purpose to help other people, especially Women. I was only willing to speak of my situation with a small group of people at this time. Of course, the problem was obvious to some residents; therefore I shared the experience to a group of four people. Individuals who appear to be strong should be cautious when choosing the right persons or groups to receive counsel and discuss their situations. I did not seek compassion, but rather showed respect to those to whom I felt accountable. I had no desire whatsoever to run from my ordeal. I wanted to stand and find strength and health and experience a rich and happy life to lead the community that I was called to guide. My strength came from a prayer and praise life that I adopted before my experiences. In all of these phases the mercies and faithfulness of God's promise was extended to us.

These principles are ways to find a quick source to overcome trials, reevaluate problems, forgive, exercise compassion for a lost friend, use the power of faith, focus on the good, and make others happy through sharing. I could not forgive and be compassionate, if I did not use the concept of Faith in God. Faith is the quality of things hope for, the evidence of things not seen. There are no witnesses in order to receive (Heb. 11; 1). These basic rules that I adopted derived from my faith in God.

My strong awareness of God compelled me to believe that God was with me in the fires of my battles. The Almighty was not only with me, but the assurance that he would bring me out was concrete. I understand that faith in God and practicing the discipline of fasting helps to destroy negative thoughts and practices in our lives. When Christians fast, we receive confidence in God to be victorious in times of testing Richard J. Foster in *Celebrating of Discipline* claims, "How easily we allow the unwanted to take precedence. How quickly we desire things we do not need until we are confined to them (Foster J. 1998, 56)". The discipline of fasting is carried out when a believer sees himself in need of more power from God to overcome and do God's work. When Christians fast, their faith grows stronger in God and many of their petitions are granted, according to the will of God. Then after one's request has been granted it is important to help other people who are in need.

CHAPTER THREE

Fact I: Conquering The Loss Of An Intimate Friend

My Experience

It is of great necessity that people know what bond they are going to build with another person. In life a relationship could have all the right elements for lasting and still turn out to be a failure. A loved one who was faithful and loving can pass from this life, leaving matters unresolved. However, death is unavoidable. In some cases, a friend can break a bond, because of mistrust, or other reasons. In building a relationship with someone, whether it is with a friend, relative, spouse or child, you are giving part of your very own self to that individual. There are things that you both have done together, even in making sacrifices. Some things that you shared with that very close friend, you would not disclose it to others. This can be called trust. Relationships call for work, commitment and understanding, among other things. To become mutual friends, it is imperative that each individual respects the other's feelings

When so many different kinds of sacrifices are made to form a connection, it is very hard to bear the end of a commitment. Sometimes the breaking off of a relationship can be good. In my view, we can build partnerships that are illegal and not right for us in the sight of God (2 Cor. 6:14). Nevertheless, in all kinds of disappointments, breakups, and deaths, we must strive to be consoled, knowing there are possibilities of better circumstances. Whether the closeness of that friend was meant to exist or not, face it with hope and you will triumph. Trials are not forever; they will pass, by God's grace. Take courage and hope. Your hard ordeal can bring much precious gain in the lives of many hopeless people. In return your very own life can experience an eternity of fruitfulness. One day you can awake to some dilemmas and in a couple of days those same crises can have great substances.

PHASE 1:

FELT AS IF A DEAD WAS TAKEN OUT OF THE HOUSE?

When you are experiencing grief and sadness then immediately comes a feeling of detachment. With the feeling of "My partner left and is not returning" You go to sleep with your mind packed with feelings of shame, confusion, and disappointment. To your amazement, just as you are awake in the morning, you can feel all of the ordeal and its confusion packed in your forehead.

PRINCIPLE 1:

FIND A QUICK SOURCE

Cry aloud to the closest person who is next to you who have some compassion. The best person is God.

Say, "God keep me in my right mind." Remain positive that you are going feel better in your head. Immediately, burst out into thanksgiving to God, for being alive.

Continue for a steady ten fifteen minutes or more in praises and thanksgiving, remembering people who have done good deeds unto you.

Let praises to God be a daily routine. You will find other things to say during the course of Thanksgiving.

PHASE 2:

NEXT DAY HEAD TRUAMA

The head is feeling distressed as you awake.

You feel like you want to cry and may burst into tears.

Still, you remain in a state of shock and questioning.

Feelings of loneliness are present off and on.

Taking a little time to think over the problem, you almost neglect to do your chores.

PRINCIPLE 2:

DEALING WITH THE ORDEAL

Repeat the principles that are written in *rule one*. Cry aloud to God and give thanks as you awake.

Remain hopeful, believing that something good will still happen. Talk the matter over with someone who is honest and cares for you.

Believe your dear friend will soon return. Resist and fight against any negative feelings, in spite of the experience.

Be positive and strong and do your chores.

PHASE 3:

THE FEELINGS OF RESENTMENT AND HURT

The thought that you are the cause for your intimate friend's leaving begins to run through your mind. A sensation of remorse rolls inside of you.

In your core, you experience brokenness and hurt at the same time.

You begin to really feel alone, yet a ray of hope starts to glimmer- because you are doing the right things, such as praying and being positive.

PRINCIPLE 3:

REEVALUATING THE PROBLEM

Stay hopeful and revaluate the problem. Take an honest look into the matter and see if you are really the cause of the ordeal.

You may not be the prime suspect or even be at fault. However, if you are the offender and it is possible to reach your friend, do so.

Confess that you are sorry. Ask for his or her forgiveness. You may or may not receive a welcoming and genuine response at first.

If the individual is not reachable in any way, tell your confidant that you attempted to reconcile and did not succeed.

PHASE 4:

EMPTINESS AND HURT

It is not impossible for feelings of emptiness, anger, and abandonment to show up in this situation, but they are traps for a long stay of depression.

Resentment toward your friend who is separated from you may appear when you feel forsaken.

Continue to put the puzzle together, even though you can't find an answer.

The question remains: Why did my friend leave?

PRINCIPLE 4:

FORGIVENESS

The answer to the above feelings in *Phase Four* comes down to "resisting the traps of emptiness, resentment, anger, and abandonment.

Work against them seriously by forgiving the person who has left you.

The more you work to avoid the feelings, the sooner you will experience healing in your mind, spirit, and body.

Use a positive and strong phrase of refrain as often as the bad thoughts come to your mind. Speak out loud and say, "I am a winner. I am winning in this."

PHASE 5:

REALIZING THE LONG HALL AND BLAMING OTHERS

You are in a state in which you feel love for your close friend again.

You think, "My friend/partner is not capable of this act. Someone else is the instigator.

He or she is weak and has been coerced into this dreadful separation.

My friend is not in his/her right mind.

He/she has gone crazy-

Someone did it to him/her."

PRINCIPLE 5:

COMPASSION FOR THE LOST INTIMATE FRIEND

Compassion has now set in, and a feeling of love follows the mind and the spirit.

You have opened your soul to healing and recovery.

Be realistic and face the reality of the problem.

The act really took place. Your friend has left you.

Be at peace and be hopeful, whether you were the unfaithful one or not.

Say the refrain, "I am a winner," and add, "I have peace."

Practice singing good songs, reading God's word and praying daily.

PHASE 6:

SPIRIT AND SELF ARE QUICKENED

You rise with a new aspiration to lift yourself-esteem.

You have thoughts of taking on responsibilities for the lost partner and making things happen. The assurance of making it through life in the absence of your partner feels somewhat sealed and settled.

You find ways to improve home, self, and family.

PRINCIPLE 6:

USING THE POWER OF FAITH

The rise to action, such as earning additional and honest income to meet the demands of the home, has begun.

Depend only on God's mercies and strength.

It could be a struggle at the outset. The mind is in a position for success, no matter how impossible the situation is.

Plans have been set in motion, and sacrifice and labor are in full gear.

You are marching to a new horizon.

PHASE 7:

A NEW LIFE WITH HEALING AND ADJUSTMENT

You are conscious of the fact that you have faced a problem.

Avoid thoughts of the past whenever they come to mind.

You begin to sleep without disturbance and adjust to your new life and routine.

The past ordeal is behind, and a busy life is the day's routine with God, people, education, work, and more.

PRINCIPLE 7:

FOCUSING ON THE GOOD, MAKING OTHERS HAPPY

Focusing on the good things allows you to abandon the evil of the past relationship.

Don't give up your praise to God; remember where you were in your distress.

Work in your community, to help others find strength, joy and a better life.

Give, and it shall be given unto you. Join a Christian Fellows Church. Be a disciple of Christ, and find everlasting life.

CHAPTER FOUR

Fact II: Turning An Abandoned House Into Income

My Experience

In the midst of the ordeal I joined two Susus. A Susu is a group of people who come together and pool a certain amount of money weekly or biweekly. The accumulated designated money is then passed on to one individual each week. The same method is used each week or biweekly, until every person receives the collected amount of money. Bernard Thompson in the writing of *Good Samaritan's*

Faith says, "Caring Christians who are faithfully applying Scriptures to their lives on a daily basis will never exhaust caring ministries (Thompson 1994, 166)."

It was indeed people who were faithful in the ministry who found the lending hand program. I joined two of them and collected over four thousand dollars in one drawing. This money enabled me to hire a contractor to work on unfinished areas of my home. When that money was gone, I received a card in the mail from Discover. During that time I was reluctant to use the card. There was uncertainty in my mind about whether or not the card was real. I quickly learned that it was real. The five thousand dollars that was sent to me was truly an answer to my prayers from God in meeting my financial needs. When I had to fix the water main unexpected, I was able to charge $3000 on the Discover card. I also had a credit card for six thousand dollars sent to me by American Express which allowed me to purchase materials that I could pay for each month.

In the space of one year, I had three renters, including my own family members. In 1998, after graduating from Audrey Cohen College, I felt the need to take on a part time job of teaching in the public school system.

During my teaching and pastoral experience, I felt and saw the need to have a home that would be more accommodating for a mission. The Lord helped me to use the house and my jobs to go forward with the purchase of another house. That first residence was also used to acquire a loan for my organization. In 2006, the second house brought multiplication in three different ways. The increased finances from the second home came when I refinanced the property. I made half of the contribution to my Church organization and with the other half, I purchased two inexpensive properties. This unfinished, once-abandoned dwelling brought income and other residences.

PHASE 1:

COUNTING THE COST

Have a purpose when purchasing a home.

Believe you can buy and own a home.

Target your area for the price you can afford.

Get to know tax brackets in towns and zones.

Shop around for your house.

Spend money wisely as to reach your goal.

PRINCIPLE 1

PURCHASE THE CHEAPEST AND THE BEST

Speak with more than one broker before deciding.

Stay away from burdensome loans.

Work toward your financial goals.

Seek help from your family and friends, if needed.

Do not settle for the first house that you see.

Keep in mind that you must repay those who give you loans.

Do not borrow above your means.

PHASE 2:

OBTAIN KNOWLEDGE ON HOUSING

You must get to know the laws and rules of the government.

Become acquainted with the requirements for housing in your area.

There can be different laws for different boroughs, states and towns.

PRINCIPLE 2

WORK WITHIN THE LAW

Consult with an architect before proceeding to work.

Look for the right contractors for the job.

You will need to have an understanding of what the work entails.

Understand the necessary permits to perform work.

Work with contractor to obtain permits in a timely manner.

PHASE 3:

COMMUNICATE WITH YOUR WORKING PROFESSIONAL

Your contractor will know when to begin the process of work.

In the meantime, your architect will be processing the the work for completion, and make any necessary changes.

PRINCIPLE 3:

IS YOUR OCCUPANCY RIGHT

If your occupancy is in accordance with the state, you may choose to dwell in your house.

You can save yourself from incurring further expenses.

A relative or an honest friend who needs shelter can assist you with money.

PHASE 4:

NEEDING HELP TO COMPLETE THE BUILDING

Look ahead of the expenses.

As the work progresses, you may have the need for more money.

You may never have the answer to the question, *where do I turn?*

Look for a group that is conducting a lending hand program.

PRINCIPLE 4:

LOOKING IN THE RIGHT DIRECTION

Strive to be hired for a part time job, or create something for yourself.

Seek reasonable credit, if you can.

Repay your loan as you agreed to do.

If you can find the groups with Susus, become a member of two

Joining two groups will allow you to receive a larger sum of money.

PHASE 5:

DO NOT OVERWORK

Body and mind can become drained.

Resources can become drained.

Bear in mind you are limited in power and strength

Guard yourself against anxiety and frustration.

Sometimes the process can seem long, even when it is not really so, when compared with other circumstances.

PRINCIPLES 5:

HAVE A DIVINE SOURCE

Considering roadblocks, you must connect to the higher power, which is God almighty and his Son.

Give thanks for what you have already accomplished.

Prayer helps to relax the tension of the mind.

Take time out to rest and live a normal life.

PHASE 6

LOOK INTO THE EQUITY OF THE HOUSE

See that your house is well kept!

Inquire into the value of your house.

PRINCIPLES 6:

THINK ABOUT MAKING OTHER INCOME

Seek out reputable companies and banks that give loans.

Get counseling regarding bad loans and good loans.

Bad loans are a possibility, depending on terms, interest, and rates.

You are in a position to own more than one or two homes.

Secure a loan that is right for you.

Your house and your job can be used for collateral.

PHASE 7:

SECOND SEARCH FOR HOUSES IN FORECLOSURE

Use the Internet and its search engines such as Google and others.

Check in your own vicinity or borough.

Travel to out-of-state court houses and auctions.

PRINCPLE 7:

PURCHASING YOUR HOUSE

Look for the best and lowest price with good potential in a reasonable location where prices are not too low.

Rental income is a plus.

Have someone or a reputable company to manage your buildings.

This method can relieve some unnecessary stress.

CHAPTER FIVE

Fact III: Being An Honor Student, Even When Disapproved

My Experience

Be strong if you had a good start but at some point you are disapproved. In 1997, I began my graduate study. After passing the entrance exam, I received a presidential scholarship. My tuition was reduced by one thousand dollars for one semester, but I lost it at the end of the semester.

When I entered the program, I had all confidence that I would do well from start to finish. At the commencement of the program, I worked as an intern in a congressman's office in Brooklyn, New York, assisting the liaison. The course was based on organization, from vision to mission and the entirety of business.

It was two weeks before the first semester closed when the dean and instructor realized that my best platform for writing on organization was from my very own perspective and not from another. I had yearned to write from my own experience from the very first night of college. I was given the opportunity to begin the work all over, and there was a test to be taken at the same time. I did not do well on the test, but I understood the balance of course work. My perseverance was high to obtain a good grade.

Because I wanted to pass and do well, I thought my busy schedule with my ministry work would not allow me to complete my schoolwork on time. It was the age of the word processor and the beginning of the computer age. To be assured that I had it right for test, I wrote the work and sent it from my home in Brooklyn to someone in Queens to be typed. When I received it, there were too many typographical errors. I only had a couple of days left to take the work in. An enormous amount of sacrifice was made in correcting the papers and returning it for typewriting corrections. I hired a car for twenty-five dollars and sent the work with a cab driver, at two a.m. in a morning.

The work was due on a Saturday, and I received the work the same morning. I was going to school, hoping everything was right. When I opened the folder, there were more errors than I had found in the first manuscript. I could not do anything but take it in. I took the work to the professor and when he read it, he uttered, "Neithe, you understood the questions, but there are too many typographical errors. I cannot give you the full grade." That paper brought my grade point average to 2.9 GPA. The lowest grade to remain in the program was 3.0.

I was called in to sit with two faculty members regarding my grade. In the conversation I was asked, "Do you think you can make four *B*'s in the next school term?" I replied, "How about making *A*'s." One of the faculty members exclaimed, "Rev, have you dealt with the demon already?" I responded, "Yes!" It was made clear to me that I was on my own. The judgment that I was evaluated with for my success was dependent upon the past.

There was no certainty that I was judged by my maturity in age, seeing as I was already fifty-one years old. Judging a Student by age for good performance might have never been the case with the instructors. However, in any area of learning, I recommend that those who are in authority must be respected for holding high standards of performance in regard to any age or gender. John T. E Richardson says in his Abstract, *Student in Higher Education,* "Mature students are often said to be deficient in study skills, but recent literature concluded…they found grown-up students obtained significant higher scores in degree course. An individual should never be judged by their age, religion, gender, or any other decisive factors for achieving high scores in schools or colleges (Richardson 1995, Vol. 20, No 1)."

It felt as though I had reached the lowest point in my academic performance among my peers, but I left that room unmoved by the statement of disapproval. There was an undoubted assurance deep inside of me that I could perform with excellence. When I arrived home, I told my youngest daughter what was said to me. I declared, "I will show them what my God can do. Let them wait." Immediately, I reached a decision that in guiding my youngest child to do the typewritten work, I would begin my work ahead of time. My knowledge of the course work was very clear, and there was no place in my vocabulary for quitting.

As the Lord allowed me to arise the morning of class, I was in the classroom. Three weeks later in the new school term, I took my work to show the professor. He said to me, "Reverend, has anyone told you that you are an amazing person." I did not make a reply, but listened. At the end of that semester, I made three *A*'s and two *B*'s with one plus. The final term, I scored four *A*'s, one *B*, and I was honorary on the Dean's list before graduation. The main instructor wrote on my final paper, "I thought when you came into this class, you were lost, but I am delighted to say I was very wrong." I was unable to attend graduation because I was too late to pick up my garments. I was told that I was an honorary, and I was also called to a celebration dinner after.

It is very important for me to caution students of all ages to give their undivided attention to their school or college work, their teachers, and instructors in the classroom. It is also imperative not to lack attendance on the first days and weeks from school. The first days and weeks are the introduction to the courses. If attendance is neglected at those times, it is very likely that students will have a more difficult time in understanding the subject work. Failure to understand course work will result in bad grades and non-promotion. Dr. George N. Reche, and Dr. Zachariahkariuki Mbugua *International Journal of Humanities and Social Services*; Factors Contributing Poor Performance in Kenya Certification of Primary Education in Public Day Primary Schools stated, "When learning begins, the majority of students start learning in the second week of school term, lots of time is wasted (Reche, and Mbugua Vol. 2 No. 5, March 2012, 14pdf)". This practice of learning commence late on schools terms has been notable to many, and should be avoided.

If when you are *hit hard* with any trying situation in life, you can still *score high* in any capacity and "become an honor student, even if you were disapproved". This is exactly what happened to me. I will ever give God the glory.

PHASE 1

CHOSE A FAMILIAR SUBJECT

You and your grade are already a challenge.

Seek the most appropriate subject,

One you can manage and like.

It must be in your course and be valuable.

Decide to work hard and be excellent at it.

PRINCIPLE:

TALK AND EXPLAIN TO TEACHER/ PROFESSOR

Make an appointment to communicate about the course work with your teacher.

Follow the instructor's proposals and corrections.

Give your undivided attention in the classroom.

The safest way to get your work done is to follow the rules of your teacher and to work with her.

PHASE 2:

PREPARE YOUR MATERIALS

Know what is needed for the course work and have it ahead of time.

Avoid getting substitute materials for the class work.

Play by the rules.

Don't take the professors for granted.

They know what is required for the course.

PRINCIPLE 2:

LISTEN TO TEACHER

Know what is expected of you.

Learn to use a computer and take courses in technology. Follow the trend of the class.

Don't fail to make the changes that are asked of you.

PHASE 3:

SET GOALS AND OBJECTIVES

Make goals for the time that the project will begin and end.

What are you setting goals for?

Know your problem and understand your needs.

Be realistic in setting your goals.

PRINCIPLES 3:

KEEPING GOALS AND OBJECTIVES

Work toward completing your goal.

Make a step-by-step plan as to how you will accomplish your goals.

Implement your plan with your steps.

Plan strategically.

Change if necessary at an early time.

Be aware that the teacher needs to know about your changes.

PHASE 4:

PREPARE YOUR RESEARCH

Target areas for research in due time.

Make sure these areas can be reached.

Know your subject area and if your topics are in Agreement with you research information.

PRINCIPLE 4:

TARGET AREAS

Places of research can be the library that is most the appropriate for your assignment.

The Internet is a good, convenient resource.

Interview sheets must be prepared ahead of time.

Find your people of interest, even if they are in a foreign country.

PHASE 5:

LISTEN TO YOUR TEACHER

Avoid distraction of any kind, from anywhere.

Don't be intimidated by anyone in class.

Understand the strategies that can be used against you to make you fail.

PRINCIPLE 5:

TAKE NOTES IN A BOUND BOOK

The very first time your instructor explains the subject, make notes.

Copy as much information as you possibly can.

Listening helps you to retain information from your instructor.

Listening gives you time to go over the subject in your head.

Ask questions when they are appropriate in class, if you do not understand what was imparted to the class.

Disregard anything used to halt your interest.

If others in class use steps to hinder you, respect them, but move on.

PHASE 6:

MAKE AN APPOINTMENT WITH THE INSTRUCTOR

Ask him/her for permission to preview your work.

Prioritize in order to have your work set in order.

Keep the appointment.

Avoid making answers to questions that are out of range.

Stay away from any unnecessary distractions.

PRINCIPLE 6:

KEEP FOCUSED WITH WORK AND APPOINTMENTS

Keep focused and work with other students.

If, for some uncontrollable circumstance, you are not able to keep the appointment, contact your Teacher in advance before the due date of the assignment.

Make answers to the questions that were asked of you.

Ask someone who is trustworthy and acquainted with the subject to check your work if teacher is not available.

PHASE 7:

TYPE YOUR OWN WORK AHEAD OF TIME

Learn to type or take a short course.

Depending upon others to type your class work creates uncertainty.

An individual can have good intentions when you hire them, or they may not.

Regarding their situation, it can become impossible to meet your requirements.

Typographical errors are crucial to your grades.

PRINCLE 7:

YOUR TYPING CAN HELP YOUR GRADE

Place much effort on both your comprehension and typewriting.

Find two individuals to proofread before you hand in your assignments. If one person is not available, you may count on the other.

Be certain to carry out the requirements of the instructor/professor.

Know and do your work for yourself. Make corrections.

Take the completed work to the teacher before the final due date.

CHAPTER SIX

Fact IV: Keeping A Sound Mind

Experience

In my search for the definition of the word "mind", my understanding was strengthened with other writer's meaning. It has also given me the opportunity to interpret and document my own knowledge of the mind. I believe that so many of us can identify with the interchangeable way in which the word *mind* is sometimes used as the *heart, brain, spirit,* and even *soul.*

In my comprehension, the mind is the seat of all consciousness and capability given to man by God. This power of perception gives humans the ability to think, reason, and make choices between that which is good and bad. In other cases, the mind is seen as the spirit. The Bible states, "And David said my son, it was in my mind to build a house for the Lord (1Chron. 22:7)". In other words, to erect a house was in David's consciousness, lodged somewhere in one of the areas of his faculty.

The Bible states, "For with the heart, man believes unto righteousness (Rom. 10:16)." The word *believe* is an active word. In order to believe, one has to use his thinking power. Editorial Board Chairman Albert H. Marckwardt (1994), In *Webster Comprehensive Dictionary* "The heart is the seat of will, affections, emotions, one's most thoughts and feelings, or inner part of something, structure which sustains the circulation of the blood, by alternating contraction systolic and diastolic M.1994, 582). We can gather from Marcknadt that the heart is the organ responsible for transporting blood from one ventricle of the body to another, and, at the same time, the heart is something that processes thought and will–it is the inner core of anything. Therefore, the heart is not just comprised of cells; it is a state of consciousness or awareness.

Many of us might have seen pictures of the brain. It looks like a fleshy organ, which doctors can maneuver with, but no one can see or feel the mind. Dennis Coon expounds; in *Essentials of Psychology: Exploration and Application that;* "The brain is as big as a grapefruit, consist of a billion of nerve cells called neutrons, carrying and processing information, activities, muscle, gland…consciousness and knowledge buried in the brain." How do the cells receive the power to give signals (Coon 1995, 42)?" Well, it is obvious that the cells are transmitted in processing not by themselves, but by the awareness God has placed within mortals.

Creating this discussion of the different functions in the mind, heart, spirit and brain, I declared that man has been blessed with the ability to make his own choices as to what he wants to do, where he wants to go, and more. We are not controlled by the neurons; instead we have the ability to control what decisions we make. The power to choose is a mortal's decision.

PHASE 1:

DO NOT DISREGARD THE POWER OF THE MIND

Every battle that you are fighting in the physical world must also be fought in your mind.

Your mind determines the action you will take.

The results of your actions come from what you give the mind.

PRINCIPLE 1:

A CHAMPION IN YOUR BODY

Your mind is more powerful than your feelings.

As you feed your body with good and healthy foods, feed your mind with things that are good, pure, lovely right, and lasting.

With God's help through Christ Jesus, you will overcome any difficulties.

Fight to win by having a victorious mind.

Let your mind return to good things.

Be aware of your change and your journey to recovery.

PHASE 2:

DO NOT THINK TO DO EVIL

The thoughts of evil are painful, depressing, and revengeful.

Whatever you accept in your mind, you will receive.

Consider the consequence of giving in to the feelings that will try to come to your mind

PRINCIPLE 2:

WINNING THE BATTLE OF THE MIND

The things you allow in your mind can break or make you.

Break bad thoughts by resenting them.

Choose the good you desire and watch that you do not take any thing in your mind besides that which you need.

Fight against negative thoughts each time you are faced with temptations.

Remember, you are a winner!

PHASE 3:

CHOOSING YOUR COMPANY

Your company can be people, of course! It is also the books that you read, shows you look at, places you attend, and the music that you listen to.

Evil communication corrupts good manners

PRINCIPLE 3:

YOUR COMPANY WILL BE THE STATE OF YOUR MIND

You know wrong from right at this point and time in your life, whether you are young or old.

Find friendship with God and his Son. God is the authority over your power of consciousness every time.

Pay attention to how people in your groups react.

Is it humanly and in the range of good manners?

Listen to your conversation. It will tell you what you read and listen to.

PHASE 4:

TAKING CONTROL OF THE MIND

Take time to reflect upon what you have decided for having a powerful mind, also think on the goals that have chosen for your life.

Choose words and statements to speak in your life.

Purpose in your mind to work toward the good that you have envisioned.

PRINCIPLE 4:

I AM WHO I AM

Write out the statements you have chosen.

Share your vision with others.

Set goals and work toward them; it is not too early.

Name and make strategic plans, step one through your desired number.

Implement your plans as you see necessary.

PHASE 5:

MIND RULING LIFE

Are you realizing that you are not afraid of facing any situation, whether good or evil?

Do you feel that you are quick to ignore the things that were once an ordeal to you?

Do sexual feelings in your body remain a challenge?

PRINCIPLE 5:

MIND OVER FEELINGS

You have the realization that a "good mind" is now in control.

By God's help, you have acquired the faith and courage in your mind when you made a choice to resist the needless cumbrances in your life.

The things that were once ordeals are now opportunities to accept and make good changes.

Allowing your "good mind" to rule you, sexual desires are no longer challenges in your body and life.

You are boldly in command of your thoughts and actions, which are pure, good, and fruitful.

PHASE 6:

ASSESS YOUR LIFE AND WORK

Count the cost of what you have accumulated in your mind and life.

See how much fulfillment you are receiving from what you are doing; this comes from your mindset.

Are you fully satisfied with yourself?

Take a survey of people who have received and are receiving benefits as a result of your work.

PRINCIPLE 6:

ASSESSMENT RESULTS OF A RIGHT-EMPOWERED MIND

In realizing the result of your mindset and its work, judge the results fairly between the past and the present.

Be fair to yourself and the results for continuation of progress.

It is good to remain the way that you have set your mind to live if people's lives are being changed and impacted for the better.

Continue in the way that you have been blessed to establish if you are truly satisfied and have found peace and a right and powerful mind.

PHASE 7:

BE THANKFUL UNTO THE LORD AND MEDITATE ON HIS WORD

Consider where you were and who you were, regarding the life you had and what you have now.

What shall you render unto the Lord for all that He has done for you?

Who really deserves the first and steadfast praises from your heart and lips?

PRINCIPLE 7:

GOD'S PRAISE AND POSSIBILITY

Begin to praise God verbally, unreserved in your mind and from the depths of your heart. Be thankful unto God through His Son Jesus Christ and bless God's name.

Make a daily ritual in saying and singing praises unto the Godhead,Father, Son, and Holy Spirit, from your heart, the Bible, and song books

Return thanks and praise to the people who have helped you in your journey to become who you are.

Demonstrate your gratitude in words and works according to your scope of abilities. You are blessed with a desire to do and the time you need to accomplish those goals.

Make strategic plans by taking different steps to reach your goals.

In regards to the outcome, don't give up. Keep working on your project.

PRINCIPLE 7:

Take time out of your busy schedule to pray.

Position yourself to make time and help the people who are unable to help themselves.

Share your experience with others. Let them know how God has delivered you from bondage.

CHAPTER SEVEN

*Fact V: Conquering Sexual Desires If You Don't
Have A Partner*

Sex is not a bad thing. Sex was a pleasurable and pure act given by God the Creator when He created man in his own image and likeness. God blessed man. He placed the man and woman (Adam and Eve) in the Garden of Eden. God blessed them and said, "Be fruitful, multiply, and replenish the earth (Gen. 1:27-28).".Jehovah God then performed the marriage ceremony in the Garden. God declared to Adam, "Now a man must leave his father and mother and then cleave to his wife and the both of them would become one flesh (Gen. 2:22-24)."

It was by this great union that you and I came into the world. I personally made that vow on the last day of October, 1963. After some years of marriage, my husband and I were separated on different occasions. I missed my family and Christmas; I was moved to tears after speaking to my children. I encountered having sexual desires, of course thinking of my husband. Never one day was I moved in my heart to violate the vows I had made with anyone. A couple of times, I felt very uncomfortable with a feeling I that could not support. There was no doubt it was my knowledge of God's laws and my vow that never allowed me to think for one second of defiance. My two separations were at his consent to travel to the States, expecting we would have a better family relationship and an opportunity to change for the sake of a grounded family. In as much that I never would think of having unlawful sex, the pain of needing can sometimes be annoying. I am in compassion for the untold number of people who would have suffered the uncontrollable feelings of sexual desires in the human body.

The Human Body

Cohen Wood and; Dena Luredan state in *The Human Body in Health Disease* "Reproduction is sexual, there are two kinds of individuals, males, and females, has specialized sex cells, named spermatozoa in males and in women, ova. A tiny spermatozoa is a tiny cell containing in an average ejaculation of 200 cells, and spermatozoa is constantly built-up…having control mechanism stimulating hormone that is regulated by a region in the brain in the activity of male and female (Wood, Luredan 198624, 327)."

What can we observe as we take a look into God's word, the plan for man is to reproduce, and the book of the human body? We can see that mankind was designed by God to have sexual desire. Ejaculation is a way to release the cells that are formed, but not without the brains' consent. Human Body Scrip also recorded the gradual decrease in testosterone and spermatozoa cells in male by age twenty.

Dennis Coon in *"The Essential of Psychology-Exploration and Application* wrote, "Sexual activity does not come to an avoidable end as age increases. In some cases both men and women are sexually active up to the age of 90 years…Sexual arousal in human is a complicated experience (Coon 1995, 586)."

Everyone has sexual desires, unless they experience some abnormality, but having the desire is not a reason to use it erroneously. People are blessed to be alive, having a brain and a mind. The mind is the seat of consciousness and no physician can touch it. It is given to us by God.

Therefore, I am humbly and consciously stating that the human race has the power to choose what goes into the mind. Therefore our minds are more powerful than our brains and desires. Thanks be unto God Jehovah who gives us all things and makes all things well.

Coon added, "It may be of course sexual arousal is produced by direct stimulation of the erotic zones, which pertains to the genitals, mouth, breasts, ears, anus and to a lesser degree, the surface of the entire body. However more than physical contacts are involved. It is initiated by thoughts and images seen…Masturbation is defined as one of the most basic human sexual behaviors, that deliberates self encouragement that causes sexual pleasure and organism (586, 587)".

It is clearly indicated that sex cells do not control humans. People have the ability to control their feelings and actions by using their brains and minds to do what is right, for their own benefit for a happy, healthy, and peaceful life. Because of our sexual feelings, millions of people, both male and female, are vulnerable to becoming victims. Their fellow creatures in this world have victimized them. People can become powerless, unhappy, lack of self worth and more by practicing unlawful sex. Mortals also suffer for the want of shelter, food, security, money, companionship, wanting to be loved, and more. Individuals have allowed some of these areas of needs to bind them into unlawful sexual encounters. You can overcome sexual barriers, as you follow the instructions in this manuscript.

God's Laws

We can help ourselves by being subjected to the laws of God. We read in the Bible regarding sexual immorality, "The works of the flesh which are seen which are adultery, fornication, uncleanness, fornication, lasciviousness and more (Gal. 5:19-21). It is good for a man not to touch a woman...Flee fornication, let every man has his own wife (1Cor. 7: 1, 6:18-19)."

The works of the flesh, which are mentioned in Galatians 5:19 are all the product of sexual immorality. Adultery is the act of a married person having sexual activity with another person, besides his or her own partner. Fornication, on the other hand, is defined as two unmarried people having a sexual relationship. While lasciviousness is described as dirty sex.

The Bible obviously states that "whosoever does these sins shall not inherit the kingdom of God and Christ (Gal. 5:21)." It becomes very difficult when betrayal and separation of any kind arises in the union of a man and his spouse. This union must be kept inviolate.

PHASE 1:

THE FEELINGS FOR SEX_CHECKING THE MIND

Know yourself. Check your mind

Ask the question, *What is my position with sex?*

Am I the right person to accept these feelings?

Am I a child or youth, unmarried, married but my partner is absent?

Am I too long with these sex thoughts?

PRINCIPLE 1:

AVOIDANCE

When you have made a check in your mind, if the sexual desire does not fit you, put the thought away from you.

Get your mind immediately on something that is true and pure and healthy. Give thanks and pray unto God.

Make certain that you are occupied with something positive that can help someone. Let the praise go to God.

PHASE 2:

ASK QUESTIONS

The feelings will return again. You may ask, *What can I do to rid this desire?*

You may utter in secret or open, *this sex feeling is a problem.*

I am feeling like it.

PRINCIPLE 2:

CHOSE WHAT YOU ARE ABOUT TO THINK

Understand sex feelings. They are not bad things.

It is what you do with the feelings.

What is in your mind?

Seriously think and work daily in resisting anything that would encourage sexual desires to prompt you.

God has given you the ability to know and to choose.

Avoid thinking, reading, and looking at materials with images that can arouse and trigger the feelings of sex.

"Whatsoever things are true, honest, just, pure, lovely, and are of good report; if there be any virtue, think on these things (Phil. 4:8)."

PHASE 3:

THE OVERWHELMING FEELINGS FOR SEX

Check your mind to see what your last thoughts and actions were.

How much do you think of escaping to experience the feelings of sex, pleasure, and comfort?

Are you being feeling sorry for yourself because you cannot meet the demands of the sexual desires that resonate within your body?

PRINCIPLE 3:

CONSIDER THE CONSEQUENCES

Constantly surrender your will and desire to do the right thing, which will please Father God who loves and created you.

Think on the unhealthy consequences that you can fall into if you fail to yield your will to that which is pure.

The after effects can be double trouble. These include diseases, heartaches, and most of all, God's penalty to the workers of flesh.

Be patient with yourself and the process. You are already walking in victory–Rejoice.

PHASE 4:

THE BEGINNING TO FILL *AND CONQUER*

At this stage you are realizing the transition.

Are you wondering how long it will last?

How could your body resist the temptation?

Are you having mixed feelings, like you are a conqueror at the same time that you are afraid?

PRINCIPLE 4:

READ THE LAWS ON SEX IN THE INTRODUCTION

Return to the writings in the introduction regarding the laws of God and prohibition from unclean sexual conduct.

Read the Bible, God's word, and any other positive readings that will keep your mind clean and pure. The cleaner your thoughts, the holier and brighter your path grows.

Then you are abiding in a wholesome lifestyle, the more peaceful and happy you become.

PHASE 5:

FACING AND LOOKING BACK *AT THE TEMPTATION*

Looking back at the conduct and temptation,

You hate the past with a passion.

There is no desire to tread that path any more,

You are ashamed and almost moved to tears,

Filled with regrets and vexation of spirit.

PRINCIPLE 5:

COMPLETE ABANDONMENT OF THE OLD PRACTICES

Completely choose to put away all books on the subject.

There will be nothing to fall back on.

If you have felt guilt and shame in the past, that's OK.

It is your healing process.

Refuse to remain feeling remorseful; instead, rejoice and be thankful. God has forgiven you. You must forgive yourself, whether you are innocent or you have any part of blame.

Completely New

If you have not yet given your life to the Lord, ask him to come into your heart and to forgive you of all your sins. Remember, we were all born in sin; none of us were righteous. Say with me,

Lord Jesus, come into my heart and forgive me of all my sins.

Set me free and accept me as your dear child. I accept you as my Father and God. Thanks for coming into my heart and forgiving me from my sins.

It's the greatest life you can ever have and peace with God.

Reject every thought of unworthiness. Confess how God has forgiven you and has given you a new life.

You are completely new. Follow Christ in the way.

Take time out of your busy schedule to pray.

Make time to help the powerless ones.

Share your experience with others. Let them know how God has delivered you from bondage.

PHASE 6:

DO NOT MOVE THE BODY WHEN YOU FEEL SEX

You get the signal, but your knowledge has brought you power by God's divine mercies.

Live in the purity of God's word. The feelings of sex are normal for everyone, but meditation only for those who are given the lawful rights, in marriage should be involved. Sex should be conducted in the fear of God, and both individual find pleasure from each other. In this life, we are faced with sickness at the point of death and other situation that are uncontrollable. Always remember, if sex fails. God never fails and love will not cease.

PRINCIPLE 6:

PROTECT YOUR BODY

Avoid moving your body with any feeling of sex.

Do not touch and play with your genital areas,

Unless you are with your married partner. Keep your hands off the erotic parts that arouse you.

Avoid secret places and hanging out with people who drink and party. Playing with fire, you will get burned.

Do not expose any part of your breasts or the private parts of your body.

Repeat the refrain, "I am pure, and I am clean," or "I am a winner; I will overcome Through Christ."

PHASE 7:

GET TO LOVE AND ENJOY DOING SOMETHING GOOD

Choose a career, if you don't have one already.

Join a Bible class and be faithful in the assignments.

Set objective goals on what you desire to do and the time you need to accomplish those goals.

Make strategic planning, by taking different steps to reach your goals.

In regards to the outcome, don't give up. Keep working on your project.

PRINCIPLE 7:

FOCUS

Take time out of your busy schedule to pray.

Make time to help others who are not able to help themselves.

Share your experience with others. Let them know how God has delivered you from bondage.

CHAPTER EIGHT

Fact VI: Raising A Baby With Little Or No Income

My Experience

I recall when I made the decision to be married; it was not on the account that I needed sex. I had just entered into adulthood. It was the norm of the day and period that many parents wanted their children to be married. It did not appear that age mattered. They signed the consent form. It was one custom that I did not cherish. However, for me, without having much understanding of marriage, except for purity, lasting years, and "till death do us part," I felt it was a good and respectful thing to do. It allowed me to have my own way to choose a profession and to live a decent Christian life, having children born in wedlock.

Two years after I was married, my first daughter was born. My husband and I did not have jobs. He was an apprentice furniture builder. At a certain period he worked for wage in a furniture shop. When our first baby came, he became more advanced and was laboring with the government in carpentry and construction. Sometimes he was employed, and for another longer period, he was out of job. I worked for a period of time also before the baby came. Most of the childbearing months, I was ill. This made it very hard for us to keep feeding our first child with all the foods required for a baby. These foods were Nestlé milk, my breast milk, Nestum, and rice cereal.

When she was just two and a half months old, she began refusing the breast milk. I completely discontinued the breast-feeding. In a matter of two weeks, the baby was showing interest in the breast milk, but I thought it was too late to give the milk. By this time, money became scarcer and I was not considering work so soon after childbirth. I was very particular in giving my child the best care that she could have; Dr. George Rekers *Family Building:* Six *Qualities Of A Strong Family;* "It involves all kinds of interactions necessary in order for a child to develop into a mature human being...the parents are there physically and emotionally (Rekers 1978,. 53)."

When the baby was about one month old, each morning I would boil water and place some in a baby cup with two small lime buds and leave it to cool. Afterwards, I would feed the baby about three to four teaspoons. Why I was giving her the lime water? I felt that it would clear her stomach from the night's feeding before she began to drink for the morning. At birth, the baby weighed seven pounds, and at two months and three months, she weighed fifteen pounds. At four months, she weighed a little over fourteen pounds.

After the baby had her clear lime water and first bottle, I held her up and made sure she burped. I held her for about twenty minutes and then laid her down in her bed. I made sure she was not wet. She would cry, and I would check to see if she was fine. I got something to eat. While she slept for a little while, I would do something in the home and prepare her bath. When she awoke, I bathed her before I fed her every morning. After her bath, I would feed her and hold her up in my arms. I brought her out to get fresh air, and sometimes I would lay her down to sleep on her own. When she was four months old, I prepared a meal made from pumpkin. I cooked the pumpkin and crushed it very smoothly. As she advanced in months, I cooked the rice less frequently. I made it very soft and then crushed it. A couple of times, a small portion of chicken was added and crushed. She was now being fed with regular milk.

I kept my doctor's appointment in attending the clinics. When the child reached nine months, she came in second place for a health contest at the clinic and received a prize.

PHASE 1:

PREPARATION OF A CHILD

A mother's consciousness of the child in her womb from early conception is vital.

There can be a possible breakdown in her body, seeing the fetus forming and growing.

A Mother's concern is spiritual, mental, physical, and financial.

PRINCIPLE 1:

SELF CONTROL

A mother must check into her spiritual being and concepts.

Pregnancy comes with different kinds of cravings for different people.

Have the awareness that you are eating the right foods, consuming the right beverages and juices.

PHASE 2:

DISCIPLINE OF THE UNBORN CHILD

Mom can make effort to schedule time for sleeping.

Decision-making and choices are critical in the journey of carrying a child.

The kind places Mother may find that some places are too dangerous to travel. Clothing and shoes that are worn in pregnancy should be wisely chosen.

Avoid careless ambitions.

PRINCIPLE 2:

APPROPRIATE STEPS TAKEN

In some cases some mothers in their early months of pregnancy struggles with a bad feeling and fainting sensation.

You should find time to rest, although for a few months, your body becomes weak.

Attend the clinic, and visit the physician.

Use comfortable clothing and flat heel shoes.

Be mindful of what shows you watch and what you read.

Educate yourself with good and new knowledge.

PHASE 3:

BAD DIET AND CONSUMPTION

Avoid alcohol, sodas, punch, juices, smoking and chewing of any kind of substance.

Practice good discipline.

PRINCIPLE 3:

PREPARATION AND ACCEPTANCE OF THE RIGHT FOODS

Prepare your foods ahead of time, if you will be away from home, unless there is a healthy place within your reach.

Fresh foods purchased uncooked are preferable.

Mix and balance your diet with proteins, carbohydrates, Calcium, iron, and omega three.

Drink water daily and walk short distances.

PHASE 4:

BEFORE THE BABY ARRIVES

Do not neglect buying clothing ahead of time.

Do not buy all of the clothing in one size.

The amount of clothing must not be much.

Spend money within reason.

Think of things you can substitute and make your baby comfortable that are warm or airy.

PRINCIPLE 4:

PREPARATION WITH LITTLE MONEY

Provide a loving and clean environment for the baby.

Make some things using your hands.

Substitute a large blanket to make two for your baby ahead of time. You cannot always rely on a baby's shower to supply all or most of the baby's needs.

Provide different sizes and seasonal clothing for the infant. If you can spare time, buy fabric and sew.

Newborns grow fast; therefore, provide two to three garments of each style if possible.

Buy large basin or a low container for the baby's bath.

Separate cups, feeding bottles and nipples.

PHASE 5:

WHEN BABY ARRIVES

Be thankful unto God, and receive the newborn into a loving home. Before leaving the hospital, consult your doctor about breast-feeding.

Do not neglect feeding with your own breast milk.

The baby's health, inside and outside, must be cared for by the parent/parents.

Consult your doctor/healthcare provider regarding the baby's diet.

PRINCIPLE 5:

CAREING FOR A NEW BORN

Receive the infant into a loving home environment.

Give the baby a warm bath each day at least, considering the feelings of the baby. Consult a physician when doubts occur.

Always be sure that the newborn is in a perfect and secure area.

Do not leave the child unattended.

Checks the infant's diaper at short intervals, whether or not the baby cries.

Change in a very timely manner to avoid rashes.

PHASE 6:

WHEN AND IF MONEY FAILS

The plan to welcome a new member into the family may fail.

It can be the loss of a job, disloyalty, or sudden expenses.

Neighbors and friends sometimes are aware of this fact.

Depression is not an option.

Hopelessness is not the answer or solution.

PRINCIPLE 6:

HAVE A HEART OF GRATITUDE

Be in the best frame of mind.

Secure your health and the baby's and that of all of the others in the household.

Continue to economize and be contented.

Neighbors and friends can give a lending hand or assistance.

Sometimes government subsidy assistance food programs are available.

Have faith and hope in God that things are going to get better.

Be thankful unto the Lord and bless God's name.

PHASE 7:

BASIC HEALTHY FOODS FOR FAMILY AND BABY

Healthy foods are a combination of fresh vegetables and fruits including fresh apples, apricots/peaches, citrus fruits, and more.

For vegetables, there are yellow and green squashes, pumpkins, all types of potatoes, and green vegetables, some of which are green spinach, string beans green and dry peas, and more.

PRINCIPLE 7:

FEEDING YOUR INFANT

Consult your doctor. During the day, offer your child a little clear, cool boiled water to drink.

Puree fresh apple without the skin to offer the baby at breakfast.

Cook and puree pumpkin, potatoes, or squash for lunch.

Cook and puree four tablespoons of green spinach or string beans and squash with a fork (blender optional). The remaining amount must not be used more than once. Omit herbs in the baby's meal.

CHAPTER NINE

Fact VII: Staying Engaged In The Good Fight And Making Others Happy

We have come to the final fact, phase, and principle. We should take notice that we have been truly traveling on a journey with all of the wonderful experiences, stories, and the things we have learned to do to overcome. I must emphasize that in order to keep the blessings in knowledge, we cannot disregard the fact that we are in a spiritual warfare. We dare to keep victorious in the fight.

If you are not aware of the warfare, it is a possibility that long-lasting joy and satisfaction will not be realized. We have an opponent, and this adversary is named, *Satan, Devil, Enemy, Liar, Deceiver,* and more. The enemy will use anything and everything to knock you down. Satan, who would work to take your friends, family, joy, mind, and so much more from you, determines evil. Everything that you have achieved comes from God. Our Creator wants you to have the best things for yourself. Eternal life is the greatest of them all, but in this life, we must fight. Refusing to stand up to the enemy in the name of Jesus will lessen our power to truly help others all the way. Coming into a personal relationship with God will give you power against the evils and bondages of Satan.

Teenage Experience

At the age of sixteen, I came to realize that my earlier years of giving religious service, attending church and being active were not all that I need to be successful. I remembered at that age I thought I was alright and saved when the Holy Spirit of God convicted me that I needed His Holy Spirit in my life. I became conscious at that time that any statement I made must be validated in my application. Shortly after I received Christ, a voice deep within me said, "You do not have to make any impression of what you have not acquired. What you have lost, I will give you more." At an early age I wanted to be a professional and a good homemaker, instead of choosing the path of my parents. At the same time, I would take any job outside of being a laborer. My father was a farmer and sometimes worked for an estate as a laborer, while he waited on the seasonal crops. My mother was a very good homemaker and laborer. My mother knew how to bake bread and cakes for the home and also for sale. She also made handcraft items for the home, like embroidery pillowcases, baskets, hats, clothing for us, and others. At times they owned small grocery store and reared cows.

I loved school, and I did very well in my classes, but there was a time that I was hindered along the path in my final class and year. It was not the end to my quest for a higher education, but rather a beginning. Deep in my mind, I believed that the profession that I chose would be used to help other people in my community. Calvin Miller in *The Empowered Leader: Ten Keys* in his discussion said; "For a real leader, self evaluation not only imperative but it is Servant Leadership fundamental (Miller 1995, 23)." In my seeking I was tempted to state that I had received my final certificate, but I was quickly convinced it was wrong, regardless of how the matter seemed small and insignificant. Immediately, the Holy Spirit of God assured me that I was new and saved. During this time, I continued my membership in my old Church. In retrospect, I acknowledge that I was undergoing self-evaluation for a life of high esteem.

Very quickly I learned that I would have good success and acquire high values by speaking and living the truth. Possessing Christ in my life, there were only desires for the pure and holy. My mother taught us to pray from childhood, and I grew up loving to pray. Indeed this was one of the tremendous ways to fight the Devil. When I was faced with persecution for my new life in Christ, I was able to find strength and courage to overcome. I shared my newfound faith frequently, because I wanted others to know that I received Christ. I never desired to live a worldly life, so there was not much to put off. Nevertheless, I was not different from those who had to put off a great deal. "All have come short of the glory of God Romans 3:23." However, anything that was not needed, I gave away–I "put off."

One of the things I willingly gave up was the wearing of my gold bracelets and earrings. In that period of time, in certain religions, wearing jewels was considered sinful. I did everything that was instructed of me to live a Christian life. This does not state the fact that wearing of those jewels and others are sinful. Although my knowledge grew in comprehending when these things can become idols, I have never changed my manner in dressing over these five decades.

My miracle of conversion was real, which prompted me to join different Christian fellowships that would enable me to experience a deeper spiritual growth in my Christian faith, pleasing the Lord. I learned that as a Christian follower of Jesus Christ, fasting would give more power to believe and get impossible things accomplished for God's glory.

The Bible also teaches that when the answer to prayers is delayed, the observation of fasting can enlighten the path and answers will be revealed. Yokes and bondages can be broken (Mat. 17:19-21, Dan. 10:1-12, Isa. 58:1-12). One and a half years after my conversion, I was opened to the teaching of fasting. After that time I have given myself to fasting. This practice has been observed throughout my Christian journey.

Fight to Keep Lasting Victories

You have read how to overcome the of loss an intimate friend, turn an abandoned house into income, become an honor student even if you were disapproved, keep a strong mind, conquer sexual desires if you do not have a partner, fight to stay happy, and make others joyful. Therefore you must battle to hold these precious blessings. The Devil stands by to snatch away your joy and bring you into captivity. Tell him, "I am a victor and over comer in Jesus' name." You must be equipped with every necessity to fight and win. If you are happy, many people will receive what you have. Always keep in mind that there is an opponent who remains steadfast to pin you down.

In the physical wrestling match of life, the competitors are not alone. A referee is assigned to the wrestlers for fair judgment. Bill Walker in *Wrestling Rules, Scoring Criteria, and More* says, "The referee indicates a takedown at the edge

of the mat, and then blows the whistle for out of bounds…
he can also signal locked hands and the grasping of clothes,
technical violations" (Walker 8/29/2012,7)." In life's warfare we are not alone. God's Spirit is with us all the way
in the fight. He will never violate our causes in wrestling.
Jehovah's Spirit will remain a true defender for us at all
times. Indisputably we will come through with joy and
rejoicing

It is the will of the Devil to keep everyone in sorrow
and sadness. If you are not happy, you will not know how
to bring joy to others. There is a certain measure of peace
you can have in this world of struggle. When your peace is
disrupted and troubled, you can feel hopeless. This is why
all humans need to find how to remain optimistic and courageous. In the scriptures, "Jesus declared my peace I give
unto you, my peace I leave with you not as the world give,
let not your heart be troubled, neither be afraid (John 14:
27)." The first thing is to tap into the resources through His
Son Jesus Christ. God will show us our sins. If we confess
those sins and turn away from them, God will forgive us
(John 1:9). As we walk in obedience to God, we will experience true joy.

Richard J. Foster *in Celebration of Discipline* uttered, "Joy
is not only found in singing a particular music or getting
with the right group…which are all good, but joy is found
in obedience. (Foster 1998, 193)" As we begin to feast upon
God's Word and yield to Him, the flood gates of heaven's
benefits will be ours. This is where fighting comes in. There

is a chief opponent who is man's adversary and who seeks to dim and destroy us from the paths of happiness and God's everlasting peace (1Pet. 5: 8-10).

Everyone who desires to have true peace, which comes from God, must battle. You may ask, *What fight are you making mention of? Does a good person fight?* Not only does a good person fight, but any individual who fears God is a wrestler (Rom. 8:1-8). Everyone is a fighter, even if he/she does not appear like they are doing something. If one keeps his mind lazy, he is combating with his mind. If the person does the wrong or right thing, the fight still goes on in their lives.

As I have penned earlier in this script, Dennis Coon *The Essentials in Psychology* affirms, "Consciousness and knowledge are buried in the brain (Coon, 1995)." I have acknowledged that human consciousness, which is our minds, is yet more powerful than the brain". Therefore whatsoever and whosoever we allow our minds to be, that's who we are and will be. Don't forget every battle fought is already combated in our minds.

You can choose your fight and name it. There are two kinds of fights to wrestle in this life. They are the fight of the flesh and the fight of the Spirit. Being that we are living creatures of God who transgressed against God and his Son, we must fight for true liberty, peace, and joy. In as much as Christ has fought for us when He died and arose from the grave triumphantly, we must now keep fighting a winning battle.

Before this life situation came my way and entered my path, my life had already become a battle ground: losing our dear friends, conquering educational disapprovals, struggling to make an income in a house that was once abandoned, understanding the combat to grow a healthy child with little or no money, living victoriously over sexual feelings, combating at all times to keep a right and sound mind, and finally, remaining in the fight to be happy, while making others joyful and triumphing in leadership areas, and others. These hard tests brought the best out of me and have surely given me favor with God and humankind. All praise belongs to God through Christ Jesus.

I must confess I took it as a pleasure to endure these circumstances for the one who died for me, although several times they were not easy to bear. I was willing with my mind to accept the cross that I chose and find the defensive armors of God. These protective coverings were indeed the defensive weapons in truth and in fact. I applied them by the grace of God, understood by God's Spirit: "God did not give us a Spirit of fear, but a Spirit of love, power and a sound mind" (2 Tim, 1:7)."

The armors of love, faith, the sword of the Spirit, the breastplate of righteousness, prayer, the helmet of Salvation, and feet shod with the preparation of the Gospel of Christ, must not be taken slightly (Eph. 6:10-18). It is imperative that each person wears all the armor, for the safety and security of your soul and to inherit peace. A peaceful life is a rich and happy life. If you are disheartened, you cannot make others happy, therefore you will need to fight the good fight of faith and lay hold on eternal life (1 Tim. 1:12). Although I have told you how to rise above your problems by scoring high, gaining honor, and reaching financial security, above all a new life in Christ is the solution for health, wealth, and happiness when you are *Hit Hard* with disappointments, loneliness, and more. You cannot do otherwise than to stay in the race, which results in a healthy, rich, and happy life, and eternal life in the end.

PHASE

ARE YOU HAPPY?

As you have been told, life is like a wrestling match. You must engage in the battle to fight for your happiness.

Oftentimes life's journey gets hard and trying.

Thinking on the hardship and toil of this life, can cause you to give up.

If you fail to be encouraged to fight and win, you can also lose the experience of an abundant life. And in the end Eternal life.

PRINCIPLE 2:

STAY IN THE FIGHT

The experience in a fight is not always a joyous one.

The happiness mainly comes with knowledge and experience to fight.

The more you desire to go to the end, the more your joy is realized.

Your battle is spiritual.

The struggles are the fight, and you are called to endure.

Each trial that you face has a victory to be won.

There is a reward at the end of every labor.

Make certain that you are in the good fight.

A good fight has its struggles, but the reward is happiness in this life.

Hope becomes brighter that at the end there is eternal life and a sweet paradise to gain.

PHASE 3:

WHAT IS THE NAME OF YOUR LIFE'S FIGHT?

What kind of fight you are engaged in?

Are you fighting to win?

Who wants to lose a game?

Life's fight is altogether more serious than a game.

Life's fight can bring us eternal death or life.

PRINCIPLE 3:

NAME YOUR LIFE'S FIGHT

Your fight is not all temporal, as it may appear.

No fight, no reward.

The fight in the flesh is temporal and brings eternal judgment.

The fight in the Spirit is the most excellent and the best fight to choose.

Think for a moment in your mind and see which fight you are engaged in.

Make another check and see which one is lasting.

Pleasing yourself and taking your revenge is the fight in the flesh.

Denying yourself in humility to please God is fighting in God's Spirit.

PHASE 4:

WHO GIVES LIFE AND HOW IT BECAME A STRUGGLE

Life became a struggle because of mortal man's

disobedience to our Maker and Creator.

The first man and woman God created disobeyed

the laws of God.

PRINCPLE 4:

GOD'S LOVE FOR HUMANITY

In loving kindness God sent his only Son Jesus Christ to us, so that we can have life more abundantly if we believe.

Ask God to forgive you of your sins in Jesus' name.

God's Holy Spirit has done it. You are God's child.

You are forgiven right now from them all.

Thank God for forgiveness, and you have now enlisted in good warfare.

You will fight and win any battle of life that confronts you.

The Holy Spirit of God lives in you.

PHASE 5:

BE ARMORED TO FIGHT

In any given race, you must be ready to wear the most suitable outfit.

The outfit must be made for protection against your opponent.

In the real battle for life, God has prepared some defensive weapons for everyone who desires to win in life's battle.

What outfit are you wearing?

PRINCIPLE 5:

YOUR OUTFIT IS YOUR PROTECTVE ARMOR

You are wearing an outfit of love, with feet shod with the preparation of the Gospel of peace, faith, and the Sword of the Spirit, which is the Word of God, prayer, and a breastplate of righteousness, a helmet of Salvation.

Faith will extinguish the fiery charges that Satan makes at you.

Love will give you power over your enemy

The sword of the Spirit, the word of God will cut down any powers that rise against you, as you obey and live by the word of God.

The Breastplate of Righteousness is keeping your heart pure and clean by obeying God's right.

The Helmet of Salvation, having your mind stayed upon the Lord by obeying God's Word.

Prayer is requesting God's favor in your life and in the lives of others in offering praises, thanksgiving, making petitions, intercessions, meditations, and more.

Having feet shod with the preparation of the Gospel means sharing the Gospel of Christ to all.

PHASE 6:

WHO IS YOUR CHIEF OPONENT?

Your chief adversary is named the Devil, Liar, Deceiver, Satan, Evil Spirit, and other names.

He knows how to tempt you to live in sin and keep you weak in sadness, depression, guilt, and a world of misery.

PRINCIPLE 6:

YOU ARE A CONQUEROR IN THIS BATTLE

God's Son, Jesus Christ, fought the Devil over two thousand and twelve years ago and won.

All you need to do is to recognize that God is with you.

Use the armors, which are the protective outfits, such as prayer, faith, singing spiritual songs, and sharing the word of God to others.

Pray to God in order to keep a forgiving spirit toward people who hurt you.

Find a good deed to render unto the person that hurt you. Love and do not hate.

Be patient in waiting for your goals/dreams to be accomplished.

Experience the joy and fulfillment that God has bought through Christ.

PHASE 7:

DOES CHRISTIAN EXPERIENCE REALLY MAKE YOU HAPPY?

Is it really happiness?

Have I made the right decision?

How long is this happiness going to last?

Will I enjoy myself as I used to?

Can I achieve all my goals for health, riches, and happiness?

How can I know I have peace?

PRINCIPLE 7:

GOD'S GUANRANTEE FOR PEACE AND JOY

Yes, you have found real happiness. Everyone in this world receives a measure of happiness. When you accept Christ, you receive his peace; your joy becomes lasting.

You have made the eternal true decision for your entire life.

It is what you know and whom you know that will bring you peace.

You now belong to God through Christ.

Read God's word, pray daily, and resist negative feelings.

Count yourself new and trust God to take you through this life's pathway.

Encourage other people to do what you do.

Do not wait until your needs are met to sacrifice and help people who are in conditions that necessitate your assistance.

Having a relationship with God through Christ, you can know that God's peace resides in your life by the revelation of the Holy Spirit.

In times of adversity and everyday deportment, you will experience calm in your spirit.

CHAPTER TEN

People And Leaders Tested And Triumphing
Over Hard Trials

Experience

In our experiences we have found inept, bad, and good leaders. There are leaders who have led badly, not having any good purpose for guiding humanity in their respective areas. Others have misused and abused their positions in different ways. They may and can abuse their positions for teaching wrong disciplines, living immoral lives, and more. Others are faithful and loyal to their call. All leaders suffer persecution, whether they are guilty or not. In comprehension of these factors, those who seek leadership positions must be knowledgeable of the post.

I believe that every leader was just not made, but that some of them are born, called, and trained. However, the calling of leadership has evolved. Each person in charge must have a purpose for organizing. In my early childhood years, I was channeled in the area of leadership in the church community. In my early womanhood, on a secular job, I was accepted in new jobs as a leader. In one year's time, I was promoted to head over men and women. During my early Christian walk, leaders approached me to be head over men, ladies, youth, and children. These groups of people varied. As I grew older from teenage years to young adulthood, it was not a quick choice when I was approached to take on leadership although I was passionate and faithful in any task that was presented to me. Calvin Miller the Author of *The Empowered Leader: 10 Keys To Servant Leadership;* "Servant Leaders are task centered, because they are inclined to select huge tasks, always feel overwhelmed and inadequate (Miller 1995, 10)". At the initial stage of my calling, I felt inadequate for the position; although I completed great tasks. I enjoyed what I did.

On one occasion, when I accepted to be head of a community of people, I knew exactly what I was called to do. My call was to help people find Christ as their Savior and Lord and to guide them into making disciples of Christ Jesus.

This call consists of teaching them to be good contributors in communities, bring up good families, possess fine qualities, earn educational excellence, and be patient in trials, and more.

From the age of fourteen, I operated as a leader of a group called the "Young Adventurers." I formed this class in the Methodist Church community on the Island of Saint Vincent And The Grenadines in the Caribbean. I traveled to the capital and sat in the deaconess's office. What happened there? I had her set me up to uniform and establish the group. As I am speaking to you right now, I am amazed at what I did. It is no wonder that I wanted to leave that church to be baptized; the deaconess tried everything to have me stay and proposed a good job to me. I really thirsted to have a good job, like that one was. However in quest of experiencing a deep life with Christ; was above everything else in this world that I could have ever desired.

This profound life in Christ that was recognized in me led several leaders of the faith community to invite me to enter the pastoral vocation. I dreaded being in such a position. My delight and pleasure was just to serve the Lord God in spirit and in truth. While serving the Lord, my passion was to help bring people to God through His Son Christ Jesus. I also occupied myself by being a faithful attendee at church.

As I advanced in my Christian faith and works, I began to dread being a leader over a congregation of Christian saints. I thought before I could answer the call, everything around my family structure should be perfect. On the other hand, the responsibility was great. After many years of laboring for the Lord, in the midst of it, I felt the deep conviction within my heart to begin to lead. After a period of uncertainty to receive the call, I became conscious that everything did not have to be perfect around me. In answering to God to lead His people, a perfect, truthful heart, and clean living is required of me. In my soul and spirit, I knew that I made the right decision to lead the assembly, because I was highly favored with God's grace to serve others. Gordon MacDonald in his book "*Rebuilding Your Broken World* states; "We know how to give grace because we have received it (MacDonald 1988, 223)". My vision for the task was clear, and I had no uncertainty about fulfilling the call of God that would bring glory to Jehovah.

Over the years I have had many exuberant times and challenging periods. Several times, the battle has become fierce, and there are times, although wonderful parishioners surround me, that the experience of loneliness presents itself. To feel alone at a few given times is normal. It allows me to do self-inspection and still continue to seek higher ground. Never a day did I feel regretful of the leadership role. God has been my constant guide and shield. I have found that when God sets up leaders, the Lord will give them workers who dare to be true and close. If it is only one, God will provide.

There is a story told in the Bible in which Moses needs help for his mission to the Pharaoh. The Almighty sent

Aaron along to assist him (Ex. 4:10-16). Moses had a purpose to lead. We can understand his function clearly because he envisioned the revelation to lead God's people, but Moses did not own the dream. God was the possessor of the vision.

The vision that was given to me from the beginning caused me to focus and reach the end. All leaders in their capacities must realize that someone other than themselves made the vision. Therefore, we are not in it by ourselves. Whatever should be done, we must work whole-heartedly, with the knowledge that God has ordains it. So, oftentimes it does not only dominate the visionary, but also those of your closest kin.

The vision to lead God's people has been very important in my life. Sometimes when a leader is left alone to lead without partners, children, and others, their leadership can be questioned. At other times, leaders can become despondent and give up. Being affirmative with the other kin is not always the case. I was *hit hard* to *score high* in one of my trying ordeals, and as I awoke, I found my head in disarray that morning. It was then in my leadership role that I was put to the test. In the midst of conflict, I was still persuaded to change many lives. Clearly I understood that I can be a good leader even if I had lost my closest friend. According to Calvin Miller *The empowered Leader: 10 Keys to Servant Leadership;* "The world is not generally assisted along by people who are driven to understand themselves, but by people who wants to change their world (Miller 1995, 27)".

My greatest concern in the times of anguish was to be steadfast in reaching those people who were in need of help. These same burning desires of the vision have not changed. It is buried deep within my soul. Also whatever comes with the revelation, I was positive to carry out my role to God, the giver of the vision.

Leading Even When Your Structure Falls?

As a leader, how can you continue to lead people's lives to victory, when your own structure has crumbled? This situation is surely not an uncomplicated one. One's relationship can be seen as a house that is constructed. If that house falls and it can be rebuilt, would you not work to reconstruct it? We understand that a leader must be above rebuke. Therefore I believe that a leader who faces reproach innocently and unjustly should continue to perform in the given areas.

To be reproached innocently is a temptation and a call for quitting. The individuals can relinquish their positions, and others can seek their removal. However, we must be knowledgeable of the fact that the greatest leader that this world has ever known is Christ Jesus, God's Son. Christ was tempted in all of the ways that we are. His principles of lifestyle were different and exceeded above the existing leaders of his era. The Bible states; "Never man spoke like

Him (John 7:48)." Some leaders were in disparity with His teachings, doctrines, and identity. For these standards, he underwent terrible persecution and suffered death (John 15:18-25, 7:46). Christ, who is given the name Messiah, was also guiltless of the singling out and did not deserve the unkind treatment. The Messiah's greatest sufferings came when He was nailed to a cross, but Jesus bore it all for us and finally give up the Ghost.

My Structure Physically Fell

When my intimate dismissed the relationship, I had the idea that people would be concerned for the change they saw, but I never allowed that to linger in my thoughts. My goal was to earnestly triumph in my battle. Deep within my heart, I did not see myself as fallen, because I knew I was innocent. I saw and knew my status in the relationship was fallen.

The Struggle to Demote

As a leader in my area of responsibility, I thought I owed everyone some words for what they saw, by sitting with those that operated as heads in various levels. To the broader audience, I requested prayers for those who wrestled in the ordeals. A good deal of time was taken up in gaining grounds in courage, strength, peace, and love. I was unaware that there were attempts made for demoting. I was not told what my charge was.

Disrespect and disruptiveness were demonstrated, for which later apologies were made. It is hard to believe that I was not moved. Others make it their responsibility to demand apology. During the crisis, my heart was just filled with love and humility for those I served and people on the whole. I could not see the people's displeasure towards me. I never made an appeal for compassion for myself, even though my needs were real. I appeared to be strong as I fought to be victorious. Leaders must not allow themselves to be angry with those who despise them; instead love them and welcome them. Our fellow man would oftentimes have the chance to judge according to their way of thoughts. A leader's duty is to be strong to lead in truth and integrity (Josh. 1: 9). Joshua was commanded by God to be strong and be courageous and he would be with him.

From wherever the trials have arrived, a person of vocation can understand the tests are only blessings in disguise and have come to make us strong. A leader should remain strong when all of life's changing situations, including members of the family and outsiders who become as a close kin, should cause disintegration.

In addition to family, disillusion, or any unpleasant circumstances, the individual leader should be supported to remain in office. They should be unmovable with the fact that loyalty and faithfulness were exemplified. That the professional has conducted and has demonstrated vocation in training, nurturing, and leading their acquaintances in the right way should be key points to remain in the struggle.

In my concept and experience of leadership, all individual heads are not guilty or worthy of the bad things that come their way. Those unpleasant things that they are persecuted for should not determine their character. Chiefs of organizations or any other representatives should rather be judged according to their strength, integrity, and courage to stand the test. They should also be proven and be established by their good courage to endure the conflicts.

Martin Luther King was not assassinated because he was a bad leader. He was killed because he had a vision for equality for all people. In my Bachelor's Course in a Movie, *Eyes on the Prize*; "Martin Luther demonstrated very good leadership when he accepted to be jailed with hundreds of students. These students protested for equal rights for education and were jailed (Movie 1994)."

Job in the Bible was a notable leader, whose name is included with the patriarchs. We are told that Job was an upright man. Satan accused him before God. The patriarch suffered the loss of everything he had, except his righteous soul. Family members, livestock, servants, and all were gone. His friends took pleasure in bringing him down as low as the Devil brought him and afflicted him; they declared; "For God knows who is worthless, when He sees iniquity…but a stupid person will understand when a wild donkey is born human (Job: 1-3:11-12)." Job was classified with the donkey, as stupid. They judged his standard with

God as a person who was sinful and worthless. Job fought to keep his uprightness, by trusting God to bring Him out of his ordeal. "God had already stated that Job was a good and righteous servant who feared Him (Job 1:8)." As leaders, we must also ever fight the good fight to keep our integrity. This is why it is important for every leader to know who they are and the purpose to which we are leading others.

We must remember that the vision is not ours; it comes from above. Hence we are broken and molded into our Holy Father's image, for God's purposes and plans. It is with this understanding that I knew I was *hit hard* to *score high*, which resulted in triumphant victories. The Apostle Paul told Timothy; "Fight the good fight of faith and lay hold on eternal life (1Tim. 6:12)."

In the end, God saw and knew Job's innocence. He was rewarded by Jehovah seven times more blessings than he formerly possessed. His friends, the accusers, were ashamed of what they did. The scripture declared that; "Job's condition was reversed and God bade them to go and reconcile to (Job 42:7-17)."

It is imperative for us to fight in faith and integrity to the end. When we give labor to employers, we expect to be paid. So it is with leaders and non-leaders here on this planet; our reward is certain here and in the life to come. Once more we are reminded that "eyes have not seen, nor ears hath not heard, it hath not yet entered into the hearts of men, things God has in store for everyone that loves Him (1Corithians (2:9)."

As in the discipline of live game matches, our personal lives are being *hit hard*; no one wants to be a loser. We must keep in mind, offenders and defenders can win out in life's journey. Tap into the giver and Creator of our souls and live and enjoy life here and forever with our Lord and Savior Jesus Christ. The spirit of hopelessness and unbearable depression is not an option. Therefore, our ultimate goal should always be to fight our chief opponent, the Deceiver, and triumph over hard trials. The Bible is the greatest book, and I encourage everyone to read it and this volume.

TESTIMONIALS

TURNING AN ABANDONED HOUSE INTO INCOME

I have seen how Rev. Soleyn by faith the early 1990's purchased a building in the Bedford-Stuyvesant location and gradually renovated it, one floor at a time. This building is a four – story home. Through the help of Almighty God with initiative and ingenuity, Rev. Soleyn is seeing the fruits of her labor. The secondary income stream provided from this property is rewarding her. This property was once her primary residence and has become an investment property.

Sharon Best

SOUND MIND

A sound mind is a synonymous with success. It takes a person with a sound mind to be successful. It goes beyond physical well being in that it involves strength and wisdom. Pastor Neithe Soleyn has taught that success is not only what you have achieved, but the road taken in overcoming obstacles to achieve. She exemplifies the true meaning of an individual who has a sound mind. Despite all odds, Pastor Soleyn is a testament to the fact that one has to persevere to overcome. You can only persevere if you maintain a sound mind.

Best,

Stephern

RELATIONSHIPS AMMENDED

My Husband and I were going through a difficult time in our marriage. I did not know what to do. I recalled I had visited Rev. Neithe Soleyn's ministry, and so I called her. She cleared her schedule as to accommodate me. We sat and talked, and I cried, because what Rev. Soleyn was saying to me, I did not want to hear. All the council she gave to me was proven from the Scriptures. Twenty-one years later, my husband and I are still together.

Thanks be to my God, and thank you Pastor Soleyn.

Missionary M. Abbott

SEMINAR SEPTEMBER 27TH, 2012
"CONQUERING SEXUAL DESIRES IF YOU DON'T HAVE A PARTNER"
HEAR WHAT OTHERS ARE SAYING

If I had received this seminar before, I would not have had my four children. I was not married. Anywhere I am now a virgin, and I am feeling real good. (Christian)

The Devil tried to hinder me from coming to this Seminar; but I am so happy and thankful to God that I came. I have desired in my heart that my life belong to God. I endeavor to live a clean life. I am so blessed to be here. I am very happy for you, Pastor, there are those in your area will never mention the word sex. The people and young people need to be taught in this way. Some of them think that the word sex should not be spoken Something it is not a word they in the Church. They have a right to learn how to keep their bodies.

BIBILICAL REFERENCES

COMFORT:
Isaiah 40: 2; 1Corinthians 1:9, 2Corithians 2: 7; 7:5-7
1Thessalonians: 2: 11

COURAGE:
1Samuel 17: 32-50; Daniel 3: 16-18; Nehemiah 13:1-31; Joshua 1:5-7

Deuteronomy 3:17; Haggai 2:4; Solomon 1Chronicles
28: 20

FAITH:
Mark 11: 22-25; 1John 5: 4; Acts 3: 16; James 2: 16;
1John 5: 4; Hebrews 11;

FAST;
Matthew 17: 19-21; Isaiah 58: 1-12; Daniel 6: 18;
1Corinthians 7:9;

FIGHT:
1Timothy 6: 12; Ephesians 6: 10-18;

FORGIVENESS:
2Chronicles 30: 18; Isaiah 55: 9; Jeremiah 31: 34;
Matthew 6: 12-14; Luke 7: 42; 1John 1: 9;

IMMORTALITY:
Galatians 5:1-21; 1Corinthians 6:18;

MIND:
Romans 7: 23-25; Philippians 4:7;Titus 2: 6;
Philemon 14;

PRAYER:
Mark 1: 35; Luke 6: 12, 11: 1; 1Thessalonian 5: 17);
Acts 16: 13;

STRENGTH:
Deuteronomy 31: 6; Isaiah 30: 7; Ezekiel 24: 21;
Habakkuk 3: 19;

STRONG:
Deuteronomy 31: 6; 2Chronicles 32: 7; Joshua 1:9,
10: 25; Nahum 1: 7; 1Peter 8: 5-10.

REFERENCES

Bassis, Micha S. (1991). *Sociology: An Introduction (Rev. ed.).* New York: Macgraw-Hill.

Bob, Murray PhD. and Fortinberry, Alicia. *A MS. (October 2012). Fact Sheet.* Internet.

Bounds, E.M. (1987). *The Best Of Bounds On Prayer.* Grand Rapids, MI: Baker House.

Bachelor's Course, Movie, (1994). *Eyes On the Prize. New York New: Rochelle College Of New Resources.*

Coon, Dennis. *(1995). The Essential Psychology-Explosion and Application (5ᵗʰ ed.)* New York: West Publishing Co.

Foster, Richard J. (1998). *Celebrating Discipline.* New York, NY: Harper Collins

James, King. (1976). *The Holy Bible.* Nashville, TN: Thomas Nelson Publishers

MacDonald, Gordon. *Rebuilding Your Broken World.*USA: Thomas Nelson Publishers.

Marckwardt, Albert H. (1994). *Webster Comprehensive Dictionary* Vol. 1

Miller, Calvin. (1995). *The Empowered Leader110 Keys To Servant Leadership.* USA: Broadman & Holman.

Reche, Dr. N. Mbugua And Dr. ZachariahKeriuki. (March 2012). *Abstract International Journal of Humanities and Social Services.* Kenya: Factors Certification of Public day Primary School. Internet.

Rekers, George Dr. (1978) *Family Building.-Six qualities of a Strong Family.* Ventura, CA: Regal Books.

Richardson, John T.E. (1995). *Mature Students In Higher Education. Abstract Vol. 20, N0. 1).* Burnett University. UK: Internet.

Thompson, Bernard. (1984). *The Good Samaritan Faith.* California: Regal Books

Watkins. Morris G. And Watkins Louis I. (1992). *The Complete Christian Dictionary For Home And School.* Ventura, California: All Nations.

Comprehensive, Webster D. (1986). *Encyclopedic Edition*: USA: Ferguson Publishing Company.

Wood, Cohen, Dena L. and Memmier, Wood & C. (1992). *The Human Body In Health And Disease. (7ʰ ed.).* New York: J.B. Lippincott Co.

Woodson C. (1993). *Mis-education of The Negro.* Washington DC: Associated Publishers.

Made in the USA
Charleston, SC
21 July 2013